# Sometimes I'm a Gator

By Pam Leitzell

Illustrated by Stephen Adams

AuthorHouse™
1663 Liberty Drive
Bloomington, IN 47403
www.authorhouse.com
Phone: 833-262-8899

Because of the dynamic nature of the Internet, any web addresses or links contained in this book may have changed
since publication and may no longer be valid. The views expressed in this work are solely those of the author and do
not necessarily reflect the views of the publisher, and the publisher hereby disclaims any responsibility for them.

Any people depicted in stock imagery provided by Getty Images are models,
and such images are being used for illustrative purposes only.
Certain stock imagery © Getty Images.

This book is printed on acid-free paper.

Library of Congress Control Number: 2014911540

ISBN: 978-1-4969-2112-3 (sc)
       978-1-4969-4616-4 (e)

Print information available on the last page.

Published by AuthorHouse  03/02/2021

authorHOUSE®

To Harrison, who makes me smile every day and adds joy to my life.

Sometimes I'm a gator with sharp, pointy teeth.

I'm not in the mood to be friendly or speak.

I just want to be left alone, so BEWARE!

My eyes are on you with my cold gator stare.

Sometimes I'm a monkey.  I squeal with delight.

As I swing through the air and do flips in mid-flight,

I tumble and frolic with close monkey friends.

When I am a monkey, the fun never ends.

Sometimes I'm a snail, and my world is real slow.

The least little thing takes a long time, you know.

Even though you say hurry, I must take my time.

The hands on your clock aren't the same speed as mine.

Sometimes I'm a bunny all hippity hop.

All jumpity-jumpy, you can't make me stop.

I bounce high and higher, so high in the air.

You can't get me down. I'm a hap-happy hare.

Sometimes I'm a lion.  My roar can sound bad.

If you don't want to hear it, then don't make me mad.

I never show fear.  I protect what is mine.

If you enter my kingdom, bow down to the lion!

Sometimes a hyena is inside of me.

And a chuckle turns into wild laughter with glee.

Then the laughter explodes; there is no end in sight.

So I laugh, and I laugh, and I laugh with delight!

Sometimes I feel like a long worm that wiggles.

I'm Jell-O inside; it's a case of the jiggles.

With a squiggle-dee-do and a squiggle-dee-dum

I wiggle around.  Watch out here I come!

Sometimes I'm a songbird, and all that I say

Comes out in a wonderful, musical way.

When the day is terrific and nothing goes wrong,

I celebrate life with a smile and a song.

Sometimes I'm a bear; my growl can sound mean.

But I'm really a softy; look closer you'll see.

I can be a good friend, so there's no need to fear.

I'm the giver of bear hugs to all who are dear.

Sometimes I'm a mixture of all of these things.

I'm the gator, the lion, and the songbird that sings.

I'm the best of them all!  And all that you see

Is the sum of their parts …

Which adds up to ME!

Printed in the United States
by Baker & Taylor Publisher Services